AF496554

NO-LUCK HOLMES

AND THE CASE OF
THE MISSING MONARCH

Written by
Steve Barlow and Steve Skidmore
Illustrated by **Nick Schon**

My name is Dr John Watson. You may
have heard of me.

My friend, Mr Sherlock Holmes, was
the greatest detective the world has
ever seen. He had the most brilliant
mind. He could solve crimes which the
police said were impossible to crack.

But there is something you don't know
about Sherlock Holmes. It is a secret
that will amaze you. It is a secret so
shocking that I have never told anyone
about it. Until now...

Chapter 1

London, 1899.

It was a dark, foggy night in the city. I shivered with the cold and wished I was back at 221b Baker Street – the house I shared with Sherlock Holmes.

Holmes was working on a case. He had asked me to meet him at the docks at midnight. And so, here I was, frozen stiff and wondering where he could be.

I knew Holmes was working undercover. He was a master of disguise. I wondered which disguise he would be wearing tonight.

THE MANY DISGUISES
of
SHERLOCK HOLMES

Then from out of the fog, I heard a strange sound.

Thud, *tap*.

Thud, *tap*.

Footsteps! Or to be more precise, one footstep and one wooden clunk.

Thud, *tap*.

Thud, *tap*.

The sound got closer. From out of the fog came a strange-looking man.

"A brilliant disguise, Holmes," I cried.
The old sailor looked puzzled. "What
are you on about, shipmate?"
"You can't fool me!" I grinned and
tugged hard at the sailor's beard.

"What's your game?" roared the old sailor.

The beard was real!

"Oh! You're not Sherlock Holmes, then?" I said.

"No, I'm Peg Leg Nigel!"

"I'm sorry," I said. "I thought you were in disguise. It was a mistake anyone could have made. Look at that ridiculous nose, and that straggly beard, and that moth-eaten old parrot!"

The old sailor took off his wooden leg and started to hit me with it.

"Ow! Ooh!" I cried.

As the parrot joined in the attack, I decided it was time to do what any brave man would at times like these …

… I ran away.

Eventually, I stopped running. As I panted for breath, from out of the darkness came more strange sounds.

TRINKLE, TRINKLE, TRINKLE!

I decided to investigate.

As I moved closer, I noticed an organ grinder. He was turning the handle of the organ.

TRINKLE, TRINKLE, TRINKLE.

Next to the organ sat a monkey.
It saw me and held out a tin mug.
Strange, I thought. Why would an organ
grinder be playing here in the middle of
the night?

Suddenly, I had a flash of inspiration.
Of course! This time there was no
mistaking the familiar look. The organ
grinder was my friend, Holmes, in
disguise. "You can't fool me, Holmes.
Not with a nose like that!" I grabbed
hold of the organ grinder's nose and
twisted it.

"Ow!" the organ grinder howled with
pain. "Watch it, Mister!"

At that moment, to my surprise, the
monkey spoke.

"Here I am, Watson!"

11

The next morning, Holmes and I were sitting in Holmes' study.

"So what did you think of my disguise?" asked Holmes.

"The best ever," I nodded. "It had me fooled."

"That's not difficult," said Holmes. He could be terribly rude. And he usually was. Especially to me.

Holmes was telling me about how he'd just saved the world from collapse – *yet again*!

"A very boring case, Watson. I knew at once that the secret papers had been stolen by a black-haired man with skinny legs, a lazy eye and a broken nose, called Colin."

"How did you know his nose was called Colin?" I asked.

"I meant the *man* was called Colin!"

"Amazing!" I cried.

"Elementary," said Holmes. He yawned. "Being the world's most brilliant detective can be very tiring."

I tutted. Sometimes Holmes was so big-headed, I wondered how he could fit into his deer-stalker hat.

"So, I've decided that I'm going to ..."

Before he could finish, there was a knock at the door.

"I wonder who that can be?" I said.

Holmes raised an eyebrow. "I deduce that it will be a spotty-faced youth. He will be of medium height and he will have yellow hair and blue eyes."

I sat goggle-eyed. "I know you're good, Holmes, but even *you* can't tell all that from just a knock at the door!"

"I'm not good, Watson. I'm brilliant! And I'm right. Come in!" he called out.

The door opened.

"Incredible!" I exclaimed. "How could you know all that? Did you guess from the sound of the knock on the door?"

"Of course not." Holmes gave a twisted smile. "I invited him here earlier! This is my nephew, No-Luck."

"Hello, Uncle. Hello, Dr Watson."

No-Luck Holmes stepped into the
room and tripped over the mat. I helped
him to his feet.

"Glad to meet you," I said. "I've heard
a lot about you." I didn't mention that
none of what I'd heard was good.

I passed the young man a cup of tea.
No-Luck dropped it.

"Nice place you've got here, Uncle,"
said No-Luck.

"Hmm," said Holmes. "I hope it stays
that way. Now, as I was saying, Watson,
I'm bored. I need a holiday."

"A wonderful idea!" I exclaimed. "We can go to Bognor. I'll go and pack my bucket and spade!"

Holmes held up his hand. "No, Watson. Someone has to stay here and look after the place."

I stared at him. "What do you mean?"

"We can't have all the criminals in London knowing I'm away," said Holmes. "Just think of all the mischief they'd get up to."

I looked at No-Luck who was wandering around the study. "You can't mean you're leaving *him* in charge?"

Holmes burst into laughter. "Of course not, Watson. I want *you* to look after the business."

I blushed. "Oh, thank you, Holmes," I said.

"Oh," added Holmes, "and I promised that No-Luck could help you out. Think of it as work experience for the boy. He's very good you know."

I looked at Holmes in surprise. "But you've told me about No-Luck before," I said. "You said he was absolutely useless!"

Holmes did his best to look shocked. "I did not!"

Smash!

"Oops! That wasn't valuable was it?" asked No-Luck.

"Of course not," said Holmes. "It was given to me for saving the life of the Chinese Emperor. It was just an incredibly rare and valuable vase!"

"That's all right then," smiled No-Luck, completely missing the sarcasm.

I shook my head and hissed at Holmes. "You told me that your nephew couldn't solve a crime even if it hit him in the face. He'll be hopeless!"

"Oh, that's a bit harsh, Watson. There's absolutely nothing wrong with … "

CRUNCH!

"Sorry! Was that valuable?" asked No-Luck.

"No, no, not at all," said Holmes through gritted teeth. "It was just the last surviving Dodo's egg in the world. Or rather it used to be. Just SIT DOWN, No-Luck!"

No-Luck went to sit down but bumped into the hat stand.

"Sorry!"

Holmes turned to me. "All right, he may be a little clumsy, but he's family, Watson. I promised my brother."

I groaned and shook my head.

"I'm sure you'll soon knock him into shape." Holmes strode to the door. "I must take another case."

"I thought you were going on holiday," I protested.

"Another suitcase. I can't get all my clothes into the small one," said Holmes.

Soon Holmes was packed and ready to leave.

He disappeared down the hall, leaving me with No-Luck. I was sure I could hear him laughing as he left.

20

Chapter 2

The next morning, I was sitting eating my breakfast when No-Luck, appeared. I glanced at him.

"Good morning, No-Luck," I said. "The amazing powers of deduction I have learned from Holmes lead me to the conclusion that you are wearing red spotted underwear today."

No-Luck gasped in astonishment. "That's incredible, Dr Watson! How can you tell?"

I raised an eyebrow. "Because you've forgotten to put your trousers on."

The second day, No-Luck remembered to put his trousers on. Unfortunately, he forgot to put on his vest and shirt.

The third day, he forgot to put on any clothes at all. Mrs Hudson, the housekeeper, nearly died of shock.

However, all that was to change.

Holmes had been on holiday for four days. I was eating breakfast with No-Luck. He had remembered to put all his clothes on, for a change. (Although he was wearing a sock on his head.) Then there was a knock at the door.

No-Luck jumped up in excitement. "I bet it's a case!" he said. "From the sound of that knock, I deduce that it will be a blonde-haired, blue-eyed woman."

He rushed over to the door and flung it open. A red-haired, brown-eyed man stood there. It was Inspector Bone of Scotland Yard.

"Good morning, Dr Watson. Is
Mr Holmes in?" asked the Inspector.

"Yes, I'm here. And I'm ready and
willing to solve any problems you have,"
said No-Luck confidently.

Inspector Bone stared at No-Luck.
"I meant, is Mr Sherlock Holmes in?"

"I'm afraid he's not here," I explained.
"This is his nephew, No-Luck."

"Why is he wearing a sock on his head?" asked the Inspector.

No-Luck whisked the sock off his head and stood grinning stupidly.

"It is a cunning disguise," I said. "He's disguised as a complete fool."

"Nice disguise. It had me convinced."

Bone sat down in a chair. "What I am about to say is top secret," he said. "You must tell no one."

"You can rely on us," I replied.

"The problem is …" Inspector Bone gulped, took a deep breath and whispered, "… the Crown Jewels have been stolen!"

"The Crown Jewels?" I gasped. "Does Queen Victoria know?"

"I'm pretty sure she does," said Bone grimly. "She was wearing them at the time."

"You mean, her Majesty has been kidnapped?" I cried.

"That's impossible!" exclaimed No-Luck.

Bone and I turned and stared at him. Was there something he knew that we didn't?

"She's not been kidnapped. She's been queen-napped!" No-Luck burst into fits of laughter. Inspector Bone and I stood frowning.

"Oh, I can be so funny sometimes," No-Luck giggled.

"What a shame that this isn't one of those times," I snapped.

No-Luck shut up.

I wondered what Holmes would do in this situation. I took out a notebook. "Have you any more details?"

"Her Majesty went missing two days ago," said the Inspector. "She was getting ready to meet the German Emperor. Her maid left her putting on the Crown Jewels, but she disappeared. One minute she was there, and the next, she was gone. We've managed to keep it secret so far. Very few people know."

"Wait a minute," I said. "The Queen *did* meet the German Emperor. I read about it in *The Times*."

"That's right," nodded Bone. "We had to get in a double. Sergeant Hard of the Yard has been doing his best. But …" Inspector Bone held his head in his hands. "We can't keep it a secret for much longer."

Hello, hello, hello, what's all this then?

"What would happen if people found out?" I asked.

The Inspector looked grim. "The Queen is a symbol of power. If people found out that she has disappeared, there would be total panic!"

"So it's bad, then?" asked No-Luck.

Bone looked heavenwards. "It is a terrible situation," he groaned. "Thank goodness we have Sherlock Holmes to fall back on."

No-Luck and I exchanged glances as Inspector Bone took out a handkerchief and mopped his brow.

"What time will Mr Holmes be returning home?" he asked.

"Er, well," I coughed. "The fact is, he's on holiday."

Inspector Bone looked horrified. "Well GET HIM BACK!" he cried. "We need him. The country depends on it!"

"We don't know where he's gone," I explained.

"Couldn't we put an advert in *The Times*?" asked No-Luck.

"That is a brilliant idea, No-Luck!" I said.

"That is a stupid idea," argued Bone. "If we put an advert in *The Times*, everyone will know the Queen is missing!"

"Ah yes, of course," I coughed. "No-Luck, that is a ridiculous idea."

Message to
SHERLOCK HOLMES

Please come home Uncle,
because the
Queen has been stolen.
Lots of love
NO-LUCK

For Sale:
Crown Jewels
Only slightly worn.
Apply PO Box 998

FOUND:
A BROWN AND WHITE
DOG

"What can we do?" cried the Inspector.

"We'll take the case!" smiled No-Luck.

Bone gave a despairing groan, but nodded. "The country depends on you." His voice was grave. "It's desperate, Doctor."

I looked at No-Luck. He was grinning wildly. I sighed. "You're telling me it is!"

I told Bone that we needed to see the
scene of the crime. So we took a cab to
Buckingham Palace. We were shown
into the Queen's dressing room.

"Don't you dare break anything,"
I hissed at No-Luck.

Inspector Bone shook his head. "I don't understand how anybody could have got in here. The Queen is guarded twenty-four hours a day."

"In that case," I said, "we need to talk to the last person who saw her Majesty."

Bone signalled to a police constable. Sally, the Queen's Maid, was brought in. She was sobbing into a handkerchief.

"Calm down," I said. "Tell us what happened."

"Boo hoo," she sniffed. "Her Majesty was putting on the Crown Jewels. I was helping her. Then one of her corgis ran in. She told me to take it out. I did, and when I returned, she'd gone. Then I saw the ransom note."

"She means this," said Inspector Bone.

I examined the note carefully. It had
obviously been left by the criminal
himself. It was covered in fingerprints.
Futhermore, I recognised the paper.
It was a type only sold in a local
stationery shop, where the shopkeeper
keeps a complete record of all his
customers.

No-Luck snatched the note from my hand and glanced at it. "No clues here then," he said.

"It's full of clues, you fool!" I cried. "Give it back to me!"

At that moment, No-Luck tripped over the tiger-skin rug. The note shot out of his hand and landed on the roaring fire.

"Oops!" he said.

As Bone and I looked at each other in disbelief, one of the Queen's corgis ran into the room. It began to bark at Sally.

"I wonder if the dog has got anything to do with the case?" I said.

"You think it could be a clue?" asked the Inspector.

"It might be a lead," I agreed.

No-Luck grinned. "You mean it's a dog lead?"

"If you don't shut up, I will do something terrible to you," I said grimly.

Inspector Bone sighed. "I'd better tell Sergeant Hard that he'll have to be the Queen for longer than I expected."

Twenty minutes later, we were sitting in the throne room with Sergeant Hard. The Sergeant wiped his brow. "I don't think I can keep this up much longer, Sir," he moaned. "It's having to eat all this strange food that posh people like. I even have to eat small black fish eggs. They're revolting! It's like eating salty blackberry jam!"

"You mean caviar," I said.

"Caviar is her Majesty's favourite food," explained Bone. "She eats tins of it every day."

"Caviar?" said No-Luck. "Caviar doesn't grow on trees."

"No, it's fish eggs," I replied.

"Ah yes, but if I knew that the Queen liked caviar," continued No-Luck, "and if I decided to queen-nap her, I'd make jolly sure that I had some caviar in."

There was a shocked silence as we all looked at No-Luck.

"That's brilliant, lad!" exclaimed Bone.

"Is it?" No-Luck asked.

The Inspector reached for his hat. "Let's find out who has been ordering caviar!"

Soon we were at Harrolds, looking at their caviar order form.

THE HOUSE OF HARROLDS

POSH NOSH FOR POSH PEOPLE

CAVIAR ORDER FORM

NAME	AMOUNT	ADDRESS
I. M. Riche	5 tins	Posh Park
Lvor Fortune	5 tons	Moneybags Manor
Ratface Rogers	20 tins	Sewer under Waterloo Station

"Ratface Rogers?" The Inspector looked puzzled. "He's a low-life crook. Why would he want 20 tins of caviar?"

"I don't know," I cried. "But we're going to find out!"

Chapter 3

It was another foggy London night. No-Luck, Bone, Hard and I were standing beneath the arches at Waterloo Station. We were watching the entrance to the main sewer, and waiting. Waiting for Ratface Rogers to turn up.

"There he is," whispered No-Luck as a shadowy figure scuttled across the street. "After him!"

I followed Bone and Hard down the ladder into the sewer. No-Luck followed me down.

"Be careful, No-Luck," I warned. "That ladder is …"

A body hurtled past me.

SPLASH!

"… slippery!"

No-Luck pulled himself out of the brown sludge. "Is this what I think it is?" he moaned.

I held my nose. "I'm afraid so."

We followed Ratface as he staggered
through the sewers, weighed down by
shopping bags full of caviar. After some
time, he squeezed through an opening in
the sewer wall.

"Quiet, now," hissed Bone.

We reached the opening and peered
through. It led to an underground room,
lit by a candle. Ratface Rogers was
fussing over a small oil stove.

On the other side of the room, tied to a chair, was … Queen Victoria!

"The Queen! We've found her!" squeaked No-Luck.

"Shh," I hissed. "What's Ratface saying?"

We strained our ears.

"Now, your Majesty, eat up this lovely caviar. I've fried it for you specially!"

The Queen looked at the sticky mess with disgust. "We are not amused," she said.

"Go on! You can dip yer chips in it," said Ratface.

I clenched my fist. The Queen of England being forced to eat chips? It was too much.

"Sergeant Hard, do your stuff!" ordered Inspector Bone.

Within seconds, we had overpowered
Ratface Rogers and released her
Majesty.

"One is most grateful," said the
Queen. "But can I go back to my palace
now? It's a bit smelly down here."

"Soon, your Majesty," replied the
Inspector. "First, we need to find out
why Ratface kidnapped you."

"I was actin' under orders," growled Ratface.

"You mean there is someone else involved?" I asked. "A big boss, a criminal mastermind, a big cheese?"

Raface nodded a "Yes".

"Who?"

Ratface looked blank. "I can't say. I've never seen the boss. I just get messages sent to me."

"How are we going to find out the mastermind behind this plot?" asked Bone.

"I have a plan," I said. "I will stay here and pretend I'm the Queen. Then when the boss turns up, *bingo*!"

"Are you sure?" asked Bone.

"But I'll need a disguise," I continued. "Come on, Hard, get your clothes off!" I began tugging at the black dress.

"I beg your pardon. One is the
Queen!"

"Oh, sorry your Majesty!"

In a few minutes, I was disguised as
the Queen. Hard and Bone had taken
her Majesty away with Ratface.

No-Luck stood by my side. "I want to
stay," he pleaded. "So I can tell my uncle
how brave I've been."

"All right, hide somewhere," I said.
"This is going to be dangerous."

Some time later a dark figure appeared. I gripped my gun. At last I was going to meet the big boss.

"Hello, your Majesty." The figure drew nearer.

I gasped in horror. It was … Sally the Maid!

I leapt up and held out the gun.

"Hands up!" I cried. "I arrest you, Sally the Maid, for stealing the Queen!"

But instead of being frightened, Sally just laughed. "That gun is useless, Dr Watson," she said, recognising me at once.

"Stay back or I'll fire!" I warned.

"Go on then," she said calmly.

I pulled the trigger.

CLICK!

Sally gave me a nasty smile. "It has no firing pin," she said.

I examined the gun. She was right.

"However, this one does." Sally hitched up her dress and pulled out her own gun.

"Are you shocked, Dr Watson?"

"I certainly am, madam," I said. "I've never seen a lady's bloomers before!"

"I mean are you shocked to find out that I was the criminal mastermind behind the Queen's kidnap," snapped Sally.

"Not at all," I bluffed. "I suspected you from the very beginning." Then a thought struck me. "But how did you know my gun had no firing pin?"

"Because I took it off!"

I sat open-mouthed as Sally reached towards her head and pulled off her hair.

"Yes, Watson, it's me," snarled Holmes.
"But what? Why? How?" I blurted out.
"I'm fed up with being good all the time," said Holmes bitterly. "There's no money in it. The villains have all the fun."

"So you didn't go on holiday?" I said.

"No. It was all part of my plan, going away and inviting No-Luck down to stay. I knew Scotland Yard would come to you. But I never thought you'd solve the case."

"Why not?" I asked.

"Because you're a perfect fool!"

"Oh, I wouldn't say I was perfect, Holmes."

I wondered where No-Luck was. Holmes seemed to read my mind. "Come out from under that dress, No-Luck," he ordered.

I looked down as No-Luck appeared from under the dress. As he did so, he tripped on the hem of the gown.

"Oops!"

No-Luck crashed into Holmes and knocked him backwards.

Holmes dropped the gun and staggered back. With a terrible cry, he fell into the brown river of sludge.

"Sorry, Uncle!"

Holmes was sucked down into the filthy river. His cries echoed down the dripping tunnels as he was swept away.

Was this the end for Sherlock Holmes?

A few days later, No-Luck and I were summoned to Buckingham Palace.

"One is most grateful to you, Dr Watson," said the Queen.

I blushed. "Think nothing of it, Ma'am."

The Queen turned to No-luck. "And to you, Mr Holmes." The Queen reached for a gold medal lying on a velvet cushion beside her throne. "Allow me to pin this medal to your chest …"

"Ow!"

"Oops, sorry – perhaps I'd better just pin it to your jacket."

As we left the throne room, I turned to No-Luck. "There is one more thing we must do before this case is closed," I said. "Call me a cab."

"You're a cab," said No-Luck.

"I meant fetch me a cab. We must go to the Tower."

Soon we were standing in the
dungeons beneath the Tower of London.
No-Luck and I gazed sadly at the
huddled figure lying on the bench.

On the other side of stout prison bars lay the disgraced detective, Sherlock Holmes. He had been washed down the sewer into the River Thames, fished out and put straight into prison beneath the Tower of London.

I stared glumly into the cell. "This is a sad day for the country."

No-Luck nodded.

"Look at him," I went on. "There lie the pathetic remains of a great man. There is a moral for us all in this sorry tale. Once any man turns to crime, he takes his first steps down the road to ruin."

"Don't worry, Watson," said No-Luck cheerily, as we turned away. "You've still got me."

I looked at him and groaned.

A Beefeater caught up with us as we passed through the solid iron door back into the sunlight. "You've been visitin' the prisoner, gents?" I nodded. "Shocking case, Sir, simply shocking. Of course," the Beefeater tapped the side of his nose, "there'll be no trial. We can't have the public knowing that the great Sherlock Holmes is a common criminal. I'm afraid he'll stay in that filthy cell until he rots."

The Beefeater touched the brim of
his hat. "Well, good day, Mr Holmes,
Dr Watson."

We were halfway back to Baker Street when No-Luck suddenly grabbed my arm. "That Beefeater," he gasped. "He knew who we were!"

I stared at him. "What do you mean?"

"We didn't give our names," said No-Luck urgently. "How could he have known who we were?"

I gaped at him in horror. "You mean that wasn't a Beefeater, that was …"

Just then, I heard my name being called from across the street. Inspector Bone was hurrying towards us.

"Inspector!" I cried, "I fear something is terribly wrong…"

"You're telling me," said Bone grimly. "A dreadful crime has been committed."

No-Luck quivered with excitement. "Not the Queen …?"

"Not this time." Bone shook his head.

"Then, what?"

Inspector Bone's face was pale.

"Big Ben has been stolen."

"Big Ben?" No-Luck's eyes shone.

"This is a case for No-Luck Holmes!"

I groaned. "Oh, no. Here we go again!"